CLOSER

A PRACTICAL

TO

GUIDE FOR

GOD

EVERYDAY LIFE

CLOSER
A PRACTICAL
TO
GUIDE FOR
GOD
EVERYDAY LIFE

INSIGHT FOR LIVING

Insight for Living is the Bible-teaching ministry of Charles R. Swindoll. Our thirty-minute radio broadcast airs worldwide almost 1,600 times daily. Along with broadcasting messages from God's Word, Insight for Living also supports listeners in their personal and spiritual growth through such Christian resources and services as Bible study guides, audiocassette series, and counseling by mail.

ISBN 1-57972-365-9
Written by Barb Peil
Edited by Christianne Varvel
Cover and interior design by Alex Pasieka

Printed in the United States of America

Contents

Introduction

Jim Elliot, the martyred missionary, once wrote in his journal, "Wherever you are, be all there. Live to the hilt every situation you believe to be the will of God."

So, where are you? Perhaps you're a spouse. A parent. An employee. A neighbor. A friend. A business partner. Wherever you are, embrace what you know to be the will of God in your life. Though I don't know the details of your life, I do know God's will for you if you are His child. Ready?

God desires that you grow closer to Him every day, that you would include Him in every aspect of your life. Take a fresh look at the Amplified Version's rendering of Philippians 3:10:

> [For my determined purpose is] that I may know Him [that I may progressively become more deeply and intimately acquainted with Him, perceiving and recognizing and understanding the wonders of His Person more strongly and more clearly.]

I love that rendering. It hints at the rich treasures that are ours to enjoy if we embrace an extraordinary faith—faith that moves in and through our everyday existence.

But this intimacy doesn't develop automatically. I don't think a person on this earth has ever become godly through automatic, quick, easy, or natural means. After all, everything on this earth seeks to make us more shallow and dissatisfied. Thankfully, this is not so with God. His plan for us has our depth and growth at its core.

As you read through this book, enjoy the journey of growing closer to God, and delight in that!

It's a joy to walk with you on this path toward knowing our Lord and Savior, recognizing and understanding the wonders of His Person more strongly and more clearly than ever before.

Drawing closer alongside you,

Charles R. Swindoll

GROWING CLOSER

to

GOD

*The decision to pursue God more
intimately and unswervingly requires your
wholehearted dedication and commitment,
but it falls nothing short of the essential
ingredient for a meaningful life in Christ.
When you draw closer to Him, your life begins to
reflect His life, and what a blessed thing
it is to walk like Jesus walked!*

Solitude is good for us. Our natural tendency is to always have people around, always have stuff going on. I love to be with people, but solitude helps filter out the essentials and sift away the nonessentials. Life kind of makes up its mind in solitude.

Chuck Swindoll

"[If] you will seek the Lord your God . . . you will find Him if you search for Him with all your heart and all your soul." (Deuteronomy 4:29)

Satisfying That Search for Something Spiritual

You don't have to look very hard to discover that spirituality is a hot commodity these days. Browse through a bookstore or flip through the television channels to discover people just like you searching for that missing peace, for that entrance to the deeper, spiritual side of life.

They're on to something, but they're just not looking in the right place. The truth is, God created you to know Him. From the very beginning, He has woven a longing to know Him into the deepest places of your heart. He's given you a thirst for something spiritual that only He can satisfy. He's made us restless, said Augustine, until our hearts rest in Him alone.

Unfortunately, since Eden, people have searched for satisfaction in every place apart from a relationship with God, and nothing fulfills the longings of their hearts. Not good thoughts or spiritual musings, mystical music or "minding your spirit." Nothing.

More than likely, you already knew that. But are you ready for a reality check? That longing can't be satisfied with godly activity, either. If you're like most Christians, you may attend church and Bible studies, sing in the choir, or serve on committees. Still, you find yourself longing to know God more intimately, to be less and less surprised at His magnificent answers to prayer, to be more full of faith and less full of doubt, to be genuinely Christian— less religious and more like Christ.

Growing happens intentionally. Whether you've been a Christian for days or years, you must decide that you want to be where God is. Forget the spiritual formulas, and fall in love with your Lord Jesus, the Savior. When you intentionally move in God's direction and love the Lord with all your heart, your life will naturally reflect your intimacy with God.

3

As you embark on this spiritual journey toward a deeper intimacy with your Lord, let your heart resound with the words of Philippians 3:10:

> [For my determined purpose is] that I may know Him [that I may progressively become more deeply and intimately acquainted with Him, perceiving and recognizing and understanding the wonders of His Person more strongly and more clearly.] (AMPLIFIED)

The Practice of Prayer

Loving Father,

You sent Your Son to give me life, and I cannot find life apart from Him. Help me, Lord, to fix my eyes on Him and to never lose sight of Him who is the center of history and the center of my life. May my love for Your Word be the avenue I take toward a greater love for Christ, and in my quest for a deeper life in You, help me to see Jesus more clearly.

Show me, Lord, new vistas and new directions, and stir my heart so that I am forever engaged in the process of knowing more of my wonderful Savior.

Find me to be the faithful one You seek in Your search for a man or woman today, and use me to share the grace of Jesus Christ to every person I meet. Amen.

Make It Practical

As in any good relationship, you can anticipate added joy in growing closer to God when you add variety and creativity to your time together.

Consider the following:

- **Change the form** of some good habits. Pray in a posture you don't normally use (on your knees, with hands raised in worship, and so on), and read a different translation of the Bible.

- **Make a "Needs List"** in your journal. For what are you asking God today? As you come across verses that show how He can meet that need, write them in your journal.

- **Reread sermon notes and Bible texts.** What point was especially meaningful to you? Why?

- **Write God a letter** that describes areas in your life where you'd like to grow in your relationship with Him. Ask a friend to mail the letter back to you in three months.

Directed Bible Study

GROWING CLOSER TO GOD THROUGH HIS SON

Jesus said of Himself, "I am the way, and the truth, and the life; no one comes to the Father but through Me" (John 14:6). The secret to growing closer to God is knowing Jesus—first as a Savior, and then on a more intimate level as you grow in your understanding and love for Him. The following questions will help you do just that.

1. Of the more than four hundred names for God that we find in Scripture, at least one hundred refer to Jesus. Each name allows us to understand His character more clearly. Read the following sets of verses, and apply the ensuing questions to each name.

    Read Matthew 2:15; Mark 1:11; John 14:13; Hebrews 1:1–3; and 1 John 4:9–10.

    • What name do these verses ascribe to Jesus?

    • What does this name reveal about His character?

    • Why is this name meaningful to you?

5

Read John 1:29; 1 Peter 1:18–19; and Revelation 5:6–14.

- What name do these verses ascribe to Jesus?

- What does this name reveal about His character?

- Why is this name meaningful to you?

Read John 1:1; 1:14; 1 John 1:1–2; and Revelation 19:11–16.

- What name do these verses ascribe to Jesus?

- What does this name reveal about His character?

- Why is this name meaningful to you?

Read Isaiah 9:6; Luke 2:14; John 14:27; 16:33; 20:19; Romans 5:1; Ephesians 2:14; Colossians 3:15; and 2 Thessalonians 3:16.

- What character trait do these verses ascribe to Jesus?

- What does this teach you about His character?

- Why is this name meaningful to you?

2. Meditate on the words of the apostle Paul in Philippians 3:2–11. How important was knowing Christ to Paul? In what ways does Paul's example prompt you to know Christ more deeply?

3. Read Matthew 23:1–12 and John 14:5–15. How is it possible to know *about* God without really *knowing Him?* What character traits must be cultivated to ensure that our love for Christ is genuine?

Did you know you face a tremendous hazard when you study the Bible? It's true. Much too easily Bible knowledge *can replace a passion for the Bible's* focus—*that is, knowing and loving the Lord Jesus Christ. This year, get beyond the head knowledge and give Him entrance into your heart.*

GROWING CLOSER TO GOD
in Your
MARRIAGE

*One of the most beautiful blueprints ever
designed has been God's plan for marriage.
Established before there was any sin in the
world, it illustrates God's perfect design for
relationships, and its pattern remains simple:
wisdom, understanding, and knowledge.
Ask the Architect to build within you a heart
large enough to become all that He wants
you to be for your mate.*

As I grow in knowledge of my wife, I increase in my perception of her. I say with my actions that I'm listening, I'm learning, and I'm open. Knowledge, when combined with the wisdom and understanding of Proverbs, fills your home with precious and pleasant riches—those riches founded on eternal values— so that your relationship won't burn up if a fire strikes.

Chuck Swindoll

"Let your fountain be blessed, And rejoice in the wife of your youth." (Proverbs 5:18)

Down-to-Earth Advice for a Heavenly Marriage

A Christian marriage is *a total commitment of a man and a woman to the person of Jesus Christ and to one another.*

It's an easy equation to say that when two objects are close to a third object, they are necessarily close to each other. Now, apply that equation to your marriage. As you and your mate grow closer to God, you will naturally grow closer to one another.

But how? We asked several of our Insight for Living family members, married from five to 45 years, to discuss how to grow closer to God in marriage. We thought you would enjoy reading their responses. Keep in mind, this isn't a list of dos and don'ts that will make your marriage work, but it's a practical look at the ways you can develop a marriage of faith and intimacy. Success only comes when you apply God's Word.

On Conflict

"Sandpaper can be good for a marriage if we let God use it to rub off some of the rough edges in our lives. It's humbling. We either learn the lessons and allow God to humble us, or we become bitter and resentful." *Married 26 years*

On Intimacy

"It is so easy to confuse *awareness* with *intimacy*. Being aware of what each of you have going day-to-day often feels like enough, but it isn't intimacy. Intimacy happens when you choose to give yourself some calm space and enough time to feel what the other is feeling. The great thing about building intimacy is that you find yourself married to a richer, deeper, more complex person than you ever thought on your wedding day."
Married 12 years

11

On Forgiveness

"It's been a strength for us to know that you must ask for forgiveness and you must forgive when asked. There have been some times when we've said, 'I'm not ready to forgive you.' But even in saying that, there's been an obligation to get to that point. We need to get there eventually." *Married 5 years*

On Unity

"It was important to both of us that we find a place to worship where we would both be comfortable, despite our different denominational backgrounds. We both felt that it's not spiritually healthy for married couples to go their own separate ways when it comes to church and worship. We kept up our 'church shopping' until we found one we both liked. It took a long time, but it was worth it." *Married 5 years*

On Praying for Each Other

"She has seen that her prayers have an effect in me very quickly." *Married 43 years*

On Heartache

"My wife and I tried for many years to have a baby. During the times when we were going through the fertility treatments, when my wife was taking all the shots and it wasn't working, we really needed to cling to each other and to God's greater purpose for our lives. Some nights, we just held each other and cried. There wasn't a lot to say, other than we knew that we have a God who loves us." *Married 13 years*

On Purity

"Mistakes made before you knew each other will affect your entire married life. There will always be scars that we have to deal with. All we do is look back to see how faithful God has been in redeeming our lives. It's amazing to us." *Married 6 years*

On Sex and Romance

"Romance can be really fun, but sometimes you have to schedule it. When we do, it's a blast, it's sexy, it's just plain fun. We have to make specific times for that. Sometimes we forget that whole part of the marriage for which we got together in the first place. . . . We sometimes read through the Song of Solomon—it's really a fun and sexual thing to do." *Married 10 years*

On Working through Conflict

"We usually need a cooling-off period. Perspective comes back when the heat subsides. We each recognize our responsibilities during our time apart. At that point, it's a toss up about who approaches the other. We both want it. We always know we have

to get back at it. Sometimes during a fight, we lock eyes and almost crack up, knowing how futile our intensity is when we know we're committed to resolving it."
Married 8 years

On Praying Together

"We pray silently for a few minutes while holding hands before praying out loud. This makes it harder to lecture your spouse or justify yourself in prayer." *Married 11 years*

On Openness

"No surprises. If you need to tell your spouse something difficult, trust her with her response. When I felt extremely defeated over a bad business decision, my wife gave me the gift of trust. 'Do what you think is best,' she said. She could have destroyed me with a negative comment, but she chose to believe in me. That's because we had built a foundation of trust." *Married 13 years*

On the Basics

"Stick to the basics: love, perseverance, commitment. Be true to each other in everything you do and say." *Married 43 years*

As you and your mate draw closer to God individually and through your marriage as "joint heirs of the grace of life" (1 Peter 3:7 RSV), may you experience a rich and full relationship in practical and personal ways.

The Practice of Prayer

Father,

My spouse and I are mutual heirs of Your grace. Grace brought us together, and grace will keep us together. May we be coheirs of that grace, not two separate people going two separate directions. Help us become partners that are enveloped by grace, operate in grace, think with grace, and release the past because of grace.

Deepen our love as we work toward our common goals in this marriage. Help us to face each conflict with the confidence that we will work it out. Nothing is so great that You cannot solve it. Keep our hands clenched tightly in Yours and in each other's.

May we invest our lives serving You happily, faithfully . . . and together. Amen.

Make It Practical

You don't need to wait for an anniversary to renew your vows to your spouse. You might want to consider these personal commitments daily as you build a marriage team.

Commitment 1: I commit to personally grow in Christ for the rest of my life.

Drawing closer to God in your marriage begins with your personal relationship with Him alone.

Commitment 2: I commit to our marriage for life and to work to solve all problems that arise.

Problems come, but when you face them with the goal and confidence of resolution, you can grow closer together in the process.

Commitment 3: I commit to be faithful to my mate in both mind and action.

Trust develops and problems are avoided when you decide, "My mate is the only one I will allow myself to think about in this way."

Commitment 4: I commit to communicate—no matter what.

Even when you'd rather do anything else, decide when and how you will talk through difficult issues.

Commitment 5: I commit to serve my spouse.

Be willing to serve each other in thoughts and actions that promote mutual dependence and appreciation.

Directed Bible Study

GROWING CLOSER TO GOD IN YOUR MARRIAGE

Marriage was God's idea, and following the design of His plan builds a marriage filled with joy. Commitment solidifies the cornerstone of the relationship, and sacrificial love lays its foundation. Follow God's original design Book to discover how to grow closer to God—and your mate—in your marriage.

1. Proverbs 24:3–4 describes the blueprints for a godly marriage. Answer the following questions in light of these verses.

   • What is the foundation for a marriage?

   • How are the walls established?

   • How are the rooms filled?

2. Galatians 5 commands us to love and serve one another. What part of maintaining a servant's attitude toward your husband or wife do you find most difficult to follow? How might God want to work in this situation?

3. How could you communicate your love for your husband or wife today?

What are you forgetting that you should remember about your relationships with God, with your spouse, and with your family? And what are you remembering that you need to forget?

Remember It	**Forget It**
Ephesians 2:8–10	*Matthew 6:25–34*
Psalm 103	*Philippians 3:12–14*
Colossians 3:17–19	*Colossians 3:13–14*

GROWING CLOSER TO GOD
in Your
HOME

*How has your family shaped who you are
today? How have affirming words strengthened
you? How have negative words hurt you?
Now, which do you want to characterize your
own home? Your home will be stronger, your
light in the community brighter, and your heart
much lighter when you allow the Lord's
affirmation of you to transfer into
your closest relationships.*

Deep within every life, hidden inside the secret vault of each soul, lies the heart. As a parent, you have been entrusted by God with the responsibility to help your child discover the plan of his or her heart. The way to do that is through your attention and your words. I don't mind being emphatic when I say that the greatest gift you can give your child is a constant stream of positive affirmation.

Chuck Swindoll

"You shall teach [these words] diligently to your sons and shall talk of them when you sit in your house and when you walk by the way and when you lie down and when you rise up." (Deuteronomy 6:7)

An Ordinary Home Can Be a Holy Place

The word *holy* means *set apart for a specific purpose*—like the linen and silverware you use only on holidays. As a place where God's truth is modeled, your home can be a holy place—set apart for His children to grow. "Our home? Holy?" Yes! But remember . . .

It Starts at the Top

Deciding to make your home a holy place begins with your and your spouse's choice to make your relationship with the Lord a part of your everyday life. Welcome Him into every conversation, decision, and relationship that crosses your threshold. When you pray together, remember the little things. Remember, too, that spiritual talk isn't reserved for Sunday. In fact, many times . . .

It Happens at the Dinner Table

In between "Pass the carrots" and "Chew with your mouth closed, please," the opportunity to talk about how your and your children's lives are different because you love God often arises. As a parent, why not share something you're learning in your Bible study or through your prayer life? Invite your kids to contribute too—you might be surprised at how God is working in their hearts. But remember . . .

It Takes a Good Eye

. . . to spot significant junctions in your children's spiritual maturity. What are their worries? Their questions and observations about life provide perfect prompts to talk about spiritual issues. These teachable moments come when you least expect them. Sometimes they're cleverly wrapped in traffic jams or waiting rooms, over a mound of dishes in the sink or at a checkerboard breakfast table. The important moments happen when you model

19

your relationship with God as a natural part of your daily lives. At these pivotal moments . . .

It Matters What You Say

. . . and how you say it. If your tone of voice changes every time you say spiritual words, your kids will conclude that a relationship with God is fake as well. Be real. Let your conversation about God be as natural as talking with them about their friends or a family member. Encourage their questions, even if you don't know the answers. They won't mind your not knowing if you can discover the answer together in God's Word. And while we're talking about talking . . .

It Matters How You Pray

When you became a parent, you decided from that moment on to let your heart run around outside your body. At times, the only way to reach your children is through the conversations you have with God about them. As you pray, think through their day. What challenges do they face? Pray for their strength as you iron their shirts, and pray for their health as you fix them nourishing meals. Plead for their protection as you watch them with their friends. Pray for them with your spouse after you tuck them in at night. The result will be . . .

Growing Closer to God as a Family

As parents, decide to be a spiritual influence in your home—set it apart as a place where your relationship with God is as real as the kitchen sink. Serve God together as you serve each other in honest attentiveness and a willingness to be involved in every family member's growing awareness of God's plan for their lives.

The Practice of Prayer

Father, I pray that You will convince me more than ever of the powerful significance of my home. I thank You for being my Father—wayward, ornery child that I am. Forgive me for spending my time on nonessentials and losing many of the most valuable moments in my life—times when my children need my affection and I'm too busy to give it, want my encouragement and I'm too negative to provide it, long for my friendship and I'm too distant to show it.

I stand before You today, admitting my need for You and longing to know what it means to be like You. Enable me to grow in character as I learn more about You, and please allow those changes to make a difference in my home. Thank You for Jesus Christ, who had the perfect Father and was therefore the perfect Son. Amen.

Make It Practical

Tell a child about salvation using a Bible and these five ideas:

- **Heaven is represented by the color gold.** Gold reminds us of heaven, God's home, where He wants us to be with Him when we die. (Revelation 21:18)

- **Sin is represented by darkness.** Darkness reminds us of our sin. We can't get rid of our sin by ourselves, but God made a way for us to be forgiven. (Romans 3:23; 6:23)

- **Christ's blood is represented by the color red.** Red reminds us of Jesus, who came to earth, lived a sinless life, and died in our place on the cross. When we ask Him to forgive our sins, His blood washes it away. (Isaiah 53:4–6)

- **Forgiveness is represented by brightness.** We start our lives in Christ with a clean page when God forgives us of our sins. (Psalm 51:7)

- **Our growth is represented by the color green.** Green looks like the new life—the everlasting life—you receive from God when you believe in the Lord Jesus as your Savior. Now it's time to start growing! (2 Peter 3:18)

Directed Bible Study

GROWING CLOSER TO GOD IN YOUR HOME

Who is building your home? Psalm 127:1 says, "Unless the Lord builds the house, They labor in vain who build it." Together with your spouse, consider the following exercises as you partner with the Lord in building your home. Hold each other accountable for the ways you plan to grow in these areas.

1. Praying for your children is often the most effective way to influence them. In your journal or in the back of your Bible, list five to ten specific prayer requests for each of your children. Date your entry, and also follow up with the date God answers your prayer. Let your prayer and His answers be a testimony of faithfulness.

2. Proverbs 14:26 says, "He who fears the Lord has a secure fortress, and for his children it will be a refuge" (NIV). How would you interpret the words *fear, secure fortress,* and *refuge?* Rewrite this verse using your own words.

3. Proverbs 14:26 teaches that the key to a strong household is the fear of the Lord. How can you and your spouse model the fear of the Lord before your children?

You don't have to leave home to find your most influential and important ministry. Talk to the people you care most about and observe how to serve them. Your ministry to your family is your greatest opportunity for impact. How can you model God's love and grace to each of your family members today?

4

GROWING CLOSER TO GOD
in Your
FRIENDSHIPS

*You've most likely known times of struggle,
vulnerability, and conflict—our Lord Jesus
experienced these trials as well. When He faced
His most heart-wrenching moments in the
Garden of Gethsemane, He wanted His friends
to draw near. He needed their support.
Let His example be your model as you choose
now, before the hard times hit, never to
face life alone.*

When you laugh at something, doesn't it seem twice as funny when there's somebody laughing with you? And when the shadows of your darkest valleys surround you, the comforting shoulder of another brings a glimmer of light to your path. But this isn't material learned by experience only—it's biblical truth! We need only keep in mind Solomon's words when he said, "Two are better than one. . . . For if either of them falls, the one will lift up his companion" (Ecclesiastes 4:9, 10).

Chuck Swindoll

"A new commandment I give to you, that you love one another, even as I have loved you, that you also love one another." (John 13:34)

Discover a Friend Worth Following: A Close Look at Jesus' Friendships

Friends rub off on you. Stick around them long enough and their likes, dislikes, perspectives, and priorities influence your own.

When we think of Jesus' last days before the Cross, we usually remember His agony. But tucked away in the Passion Week are snapshots of Jesus with His dearest friends. He loved those people, and they loved Him back. He leaned hard on them for support during His last days.

Just six days before Passover, Jesus' good friends — Mary, Martha, and Lazarus—hosted a dinner in His honor (John 12:1–8). In usual fashion, Martha worked and Lazarus played host. Only Mary realized this was Jesus' "going-away" party. She heard His words and believed the impossible—He was going to die. While the others lived in denial, Mary did what only a friend could do: she grieved.

Taking fragrant burial oil worth a full year's salary, Mary lavished it on Jesus' feet. Her sacrifice seemed small in light of what she knew He was about to do for her. She would not always have Him there, so she did all she could for Him at this difficult time. Days later, Jesus would be stripped of everything except for the fragrance of Mary's friendship, still clinging to Him as He hung on the cross.

Jesus' friendship with Peter probably kept Jesus smiling. He knew what was ahead for His friend. So when Peter denied, Jesus prayed. When Peter failed, Jesus forgave. And when Jesus suffered, Peter followed . . . from a distance, for sure, but he followed. That faithfulness, born from Jesus' forgiveness, would set the pattern of his life.

Of course, Jesus had many more snapshots in His album from that last week: His friend John, as he stood with His mother by the side of the cross (John 19:26–27). Joseph of Arimethea and Nicodemus, as

25

they took down His broken body from the cross (John 19:38–40). Mary Magdalene, who came so early on the first day to bury His body (John 20:1). And then, of course, there were Peter and John, Jesus' closest friends, who ran at full speed to get to Jesus' empty tomb that first Easter morning (John 20:2–4). They came to protect their Friend's body, yet they left in awe when they realized the miracle of His resurrection. John later wrote of their experience in his gospel:

> Simon Peter also came, following [John], and entered the tomb; and he saw the linen wrappings lying there, and the face-cloth which had been on His head, not lying with the linen wrappings, but rolled up in a place by itself. . . . *[They] saw and believed.* (John 20:6–8, emphasis added)

Each friend responded to Jesus, not out of religious obligation, but out of committed love. Jesus had rubbed off on them. A few weeks later, after Jesus' ascension, Acts 4:13 says the following of the men in the temple:

> When they saw the courage of Peter and John and realized that they were unschooled, ordinary men, they were astonished and they took note that these men had been with Jesus" (NIV).

So, the question remains: Has Jesus' life rubbed off on you? Just as the men in the temple noticed a difference in Peter and John, will your friends notice a difference in you when you've spent time with Jesus?

The Practice of Prayer

Father,

Your Son calls me His friend when I follow Him in obedience. How amazing this is—to be considered Your friend! I want nothing more than to walk with Him and to surrender to Him as my Lord.

Teach me what it means to lay down my life for my friends. Give me a fierce commitment to their good. Make me willing to lend a listening ear and a helping hand, and impart to me the urgency of prayer on their behalf. Give me a sensitive heart to feel the raw edge of their aches and an open heart toward those different than me who struggle with things that have never been my particular battle. Help me to see my friends through kind and patient eyes, and help them always to walk in closer fellowship with You.

Bind our hearts together, like the examples of our Lord and the men and women who walked with Him on earth, of Jonathan and David, of Ruth and Naomi. Together, may we grow closer to You than we would have alone. To You, the greatest Friend of all eternity, I surrender my life. Amen.

Make It Practical

Want to be a godly friend? Ask yourself the following questions as you reflect upon your relationship with one of your friends.

1. Is your *love* for your friend stronger now than it was a few months ago? (John 13:34)

2. Do you sincerely *consider* your friend's needs to be more urgent than your own? (Philippians 2:3–4)

3. Do you readily *forgive* your friend when he or she irritates or offends you? (Colossians 3:13)

4. Do you *challenge* your friend to live a pure, holy, and obedient life? (Hebrews 3:13; Romans 14:19)

5. Do you *pray* for your friend? (James 5:16; Ephesians 6:18)

Use these questions as a prayer guide, and ask God, "What can I do in these specific areas to be a better friend?"

Directed Bible Study

GROWING CLOSER TO GOD IN YOUR FRIENDSHIPS

Draw closer to those you care about by applying Scripture's profound teaching to the relationships in your life. You will add a fresh, deeper dimension to your friendships when you understand what biblical fellowship is all about.

1. From what Scripture teaches in 1 Corinthians 13:4–8a and 1 John 3:16–18, what qualities are most important in a godly friendship? Which of these qualities do you desire to cultivate more deeply in your friendships? In what ways can you do that?

2. As Paul taught the early church, we must "encourage one another and build up one another" (1 Thessalonians 5:11). Will you commit to care for the spiritual health of

your friend? How can you best help him or her grow closer to God?

3. Next to the following references, write the scriptural principle that can be applied to growing strong, healthy friendships:

- Matthew 5:24

- John 13:14

- Romans 12:10–16

- 2 Corinthians 1:4

- Galatians 6:2

- Philippians 2:3–4

- Colossians 3:13

As it does in most areas of life, your attitude makes the difference in your friendships. Consider Philippians 2:5: "Have this attitude in yourselves which was also in Christ Jesus." What was His attitude? Humility. Consider how to serve each other in love. Try it—it will revitalize your friendships!

5

GROWING CLOSER TO GOD
in Your
WORKPLACE

As you head off to work every morning, you can believe that God is also at work—in the conflicts, in the opportunities, and in the heart of each day.

The degree of our success at work can be measured against how consciously we carry Christ with us to our workplace—against how we represent Him in our relationships with others and how we carry out our work-related duties. Oh, that our determined purpose would be to think and behave as if the reputation of Jesus Christ were at stake!

Chuck Swindoll

"It is God who is at work in you, both to will and to work for His good pleasure." (Philippians 2:13)

Faith on the Job

You invest more than one-third of your life at work. Punch the clock, boot up the computer, start your engines at 8 A.M. Rest a few minutes at noon, and keep your mind and body in gear until the sun has set. Tomorrow: Repeat. Sound familiar?

You're probably wondering how your relationship with God can grow when this never-ending and often tiring routine dictates your schedule. The temptation is strong to separate your life into two parts: career—public; faith—private.

But considering how much of your life is spent engaged in your career, your workplace just might offer the ideal locale for growing your relationship with God. Can you identify with the following scenarios that intersect faith with life?

Giving Faith a Face

Your friends at work know you are "religious" because . . .

a) You have occasionally mentioned your involvement at church.

b) You've promised to pray for them as they go through a crisis.

c) There's just something about you that's different, yet attractive.

d) They've seen you endure a crisis while sustaining a hope for the future.

Whatever your style, ask the Lord to make your life a "sweet fragrance" of Him (2 Corinthians 2:14 NIV). Look for ways to model God's grace and "always be prepared to give an answer to everyone who asks you to give the reason for the hope that you have. But do this with gentleness and respect" (1 Peter 3:15 NIV).

31

Heated Comments and Cold Shoulders

Throughout the workday, have you ever found yourself thinking . . .

a) "I wish we could have one conversation that didn't end in aggravation."

b) "His memo floored me. How could he assume that of me?"

c) "Why should I be the one to say anything? I'll just get stuck shouldering the blame."

d) "This place feels like a TV series. Sometimes it's a drama. Sometimes a soap opera. But it's never *Happy Days*."

Often on the stage of conflict, your faith grows even stronger. Behind the power plays and misunderstandings, you can trust that God is in control. Ask Him to help you model Ephesians 4:31: "Get rid of all bitterness, rage and anger. . . . Be kind and compassionate to one another, forgiving each other, just as in Christ God forgave you" (NIV).

In over Your Head

Sometimes, in the middle of the workday, do you catch yourself thinking . . .

a) "How in the world did I end up here?"

b) "I may look like I have it together, but my heart is racing."

c) "What do people really expect of me? Am I measuring up?"

d) "How could I ever live for God in this place?"

Centuries ago, a woman named Esther shared any one of these sentiments. The lesson of her life—and yours—can be summed up in Esther 4:14: "Who knows [if God hasn't placed you here] for such a time as this?" God has planned each event in your career so that you have the opportunity to trust Him. What do you need to entrust to Him today?

The Practice of Prayer

Thank You, Father, for the occupation that You have given me and for the chance to make an honest wage. Thank You for the calling of a profession. And thank You for the blessings You bestow upon me through my work and the lessons You teach me through the crucible of the workplace.

Give me a new appreciation for those eight to ten hours I spend every day doing my job. Give me broad shoulders to share in the load, the ability to forget my criticisms, and the heart to forgive when I am called to do so. Help me to see the broader picture.

Spur me on to pursue excellence, and give me greater determination to do the job that needs to be done, knowing my testimony of You is on display. Amen.

Make It Practical

When you are at work, you can reflect the light of Christ's love to others as you . . .

- **Work hard.** Follow tasks through to completion.

- **Think creatively.** See challenges from new angles.

- **Speak gently.** Consider the impact of your words.

- **Cooperate freely.** Meet the need of the moment—even when it's not yours.

- **Act with integrity.** Be the same privately as you are publicly.

- **Honor others.** Recognize your coworkers' contributions.

- **See insightfully.** Look beyond the obvious.

- **Listen thoroughly.** Discern what is meant, not just what is said.

- **Respond appropriately.** Deal with mistakes openly and fairly.

- **Witness winsomely.** Make people wonder at your joy; then share Christ with them.

Directed Bible Study

GROWING CLOSER TO GOD IN YOUR WORKPLACE

Does God care about your job? You bet! Not only does it provide for your financial needs, but it is one of the best places to put your faith into action. God wants to develop your character and grow your testimony at the place you serve Him Monday through Friday. The following verses will help you learn how to do that.

1. At times, the book of Proverbs reads like a Christian employee handbook. What do the following verses teach about how to reflect a godly attitude at work?

Proverbs 10:4

Proverbs 12:27

Proverbs 22:29

Proverbs 27:23

Proverbs 28:15–16

2. Daniel's testimony in the Old Testament provides a great model for glorifying God through our work. Read Daniel 6:1–5, and describe four ways you can follow his example.

3. What "dream ministry" would you like to see God build into your workplace or profession? Let your imagination soar! In the space below, describe your dream. Does it involve evangelism? Encourage spiritual growth? Model compassion and the love of God to those who are lost? Ask a brother or sister in Christ to join you in praying for God open the doors for this ministry, and thank Him for using you as an instrument of grace in your coworkers' lives.

Your job is really about earning money—yes or no? Really, it's both.
God uses your job to provide you with the means to live, but He also intends
your work to be a gift. Thank Him for three ways your work brings
blessings to your life.

6

GROWING CLOSER TO GOD
in Your
NEIGHBORHOOD

*Those who are strangers to Christ notice your
courtesy, detect your smile, hear you apologize
when you're wrong, and can't forget that you
stopped to give them a hand. Why? Because
your example of love pierces hearts in an
uncaring world. Through you, those who
don't know Him gain access to a love they
don't want to lose.*

Is yours the only light shining in your neighborhood? Thank God you're there! You are the only guiding light to Christ that shines brightly in a pitch-black neighborhood. You're their "city set on a hill" whose light cannot be hidden (Matthew 5:14), and they will "see your good works, and glorify your Father who is in heaven" (v. 16). What are good works? They are all the visible manifestations of Christ's life being faithfully lived out by His followers.

Chuck Swindoll

"Prove yourselves to be blameless and innocent, children of God . . . in the midst of a crooked . . . generation, among whom you appear as lights in the world." (Philippians 2:15)

Won't You Be a Good Neighbor?

Some commands in the Bible seem reasonable. Some seem far from it. It seems reasonable to hear and heed Jesus' command, "'Love the Lord your God with all your heart and with all your soul and with all your mind and with all your strength'" (Mark 12:30 NIV).

It's the second half of Jesus' command that trips us up: "'The second is this: "Love your neighbor as yourself"'" (v. 31). Often, our natural response to that command sounds something like this: *"Love* my neighbor? I don't even *like* him. . . . Love him *as myself?* How can I do *that?"*

To further make His point, God repeated this command no less than five more times in the New Testament (Matthew 19:19; Luke 10:27; Romans 13:9–10; Galatians 5:14; James 2:8). Galatians 5:14 goes so far as to say, "The whole law is fulfilled in one word: 'You shall love your neighbor as yourself.'"

If you're like most Christians, you may frequently opt for the corollary to that law—"Good fences make good neighbors," meaning, "You stay on your side of the fence, and I'll stay on mine, with an occasional smile and wave from the driveway." That's probably what the lawyer had in mind when he asked Jesus, "'Who is my neighbor?'" (Luke 10:29).

Jesus understood that question's real need when He answered the man with the parable of the Good Samaritan. If you remember, of the three people who saw the man in need, only the Samaritan felt compassion for him. Perhaps there in Jesus' parable we'll find the answers to our questions too—"Who is my neighbor?" and "How should I love him as myself?"

We can begin modeling God's compassion by making stepping-stones down from the walls we've built between us.

37

Be available. Build into your schedule casual opportunities to visit with your neighbors. Never be so consistently busy that you're limited only to your own interests.

Be involved. This fall, instead of signing up for multiple ministries at church, balance those commitments by modeling God's grace and love in community service. Coach a Little League team, serve on the town council, or volunteer at a local shelter.

Be accepting. Those who don't know the Lord will usually not live according to God's standards. Don't put them down or try to clean up their lives. Live right, and they'll be attracted to the difference: "Let your gentle spirit be known to all men" (Philippians 4:5).

Be vulnerable. Your neighbors already know you're not perfect. Admit that you're leaning hard on the Lord in specific areas of your life. Confide in them that you don't have all the answers but that you're trusting the One who does.

Be compassionate. Behind the "got-it-all-together" masks your neighbors wear, know that they are searching for an answer to that "something's missing" feeling. Pray for them to respond to God's tug on their hearts, and look for ways to directly minister to them.

Being a good neighbor by Jesus' definition means understanding that your faith is lived out against the backdrop of the everyday relationships that cross your path. Consider the community in which God has placed you. Draw mental rings around the people you impact every day. Begin with your home, then circle wider to include your street or apartment complex; circle your town, and then circle the greater area. Everywhere you find someone in need, you've found your neighbor.

The Practice of Prayer

My prayer, Father, is that You would enable me to live for You right where I am, among people who don't know You, who don't understand Your Word, and yet so desperately need to see You. May they see You in my life.

Give me a willingness to be involved in their lives—to befriend them and to engage in their needs. You know my tendency to live an isolated Christian life, separated from those that still need to find You. Instead, let me shine like that city on a hill described in Your Word. Grant me courage when I'm anxious and a generosity of spirit when I would rather withhold. Convict and restore me when I would rather fill my head with knowledge instead of soften my heart to my neighbor's need.

I commit my neighbors to You, Lord, and ask that they would see You when they observe me. I pray this in the name of the One who came to my neighborhood to give me life, Jesus Christ. Amen.

Make It Practical

When Jesus likened believers to salt (Matthew 5:13), He was saying more than you may realize. In ancient Mid-Eastern cultures, salt acted as a staple ingredient for everyday life. It was linked to good health, hospitality, food preservation, food flavoring, purity, and endurance. You act as salt to those around you when you offer them . . .

Seasoned Words. "Be wise in the way you act toward outsiders; make the most of every opportunity. Let your conversation be always full of grace, seasoned with salt, so that you may know how to answer everyone." (Colossians 4:5–6 NIV)

Seasoned Responses. "Always be prepared to give an answer to everyone who asks you to give the reason for the hope that you have. But do this with gentleness and respect, keeping a clear conscience." (1 Peter 3:15–16 NIV)

Seasoned Attitudes. "Therefore, as God's chosen people, holy and dearly loved, clothe yourselves with compassion, kindness, humility, gentleness and patience." (Colossians 3:12 NIV)

Directed Bible Study

GROWING CLOSER TO GOD IN YOUR NEIGHBORHOOD

People are hungry for acceptance, love, and friends. They look for it but rarely find in it in their world. But when Christians extend grace outside the walls of their homes and churches, suddenly the community is flooded with the shining goodness of God.

How might you dare to get involved in the lives of your neighbors? God may use you to attract others to Him more effectively in your neighborhood than He would ever choosé to do so through the regular ministries of your church. Spread the light around!

1. Read 1 Peter 2:4–5 and 2 Corinthians 3:2–3. What two metaphors describe the potential impact you have on your community? Describe in your own words what these two metaphors mean to you.

2. Consider the following Scriptures. How do these verses suggest your influence on the world for Christ?
   • John 13:34–35

   • Ephesians 4:14–16

   • Philippians 2:1–4

3. In what kind of world did the New Testament Christians live? How do these verses describe the people with whom you interact in your world?
   • John 1:10–11

   • John 3:19

   • Acts 17:22–32

   • Romans 1:21–25

   • 2 Corinthians 4:3–4

   • Ephesians 4:17–19

4. Read Matthew 9:36; 11:28; Mark 2:17; and John 7:37. From these verses, what can you learn about how Jesus viewed His community? How do you think He may desire you to interact with your own community in relation to His example?

Your neighbors are just like you in that they need the Lord desperately. As you sense any resistance they feel to the Gospel, remind yourself of the doubts and fears you faced when you first heard the Good News. Ask God to grow this newfound compassion for them into consistent prayer and deeper trust.

7

GROWING CLOSER TO GOD
through
MINISTRY

*When Christians serve in their areas of
giftedness, they generally depend less on their
own strength and more on the power of the
Holy Spirit. As we rely on God, ordinary
people accomplish the extraordinary!*

B ecause everything I have belongs to God, I give back to Him a portion of my money, my prayer, my efforts, my service, and my concern—with much gratitude. I'm committed to contribute to the needs of His body in whatever way I can, with as much effort as I can. Won't you join with me in this generous and sacrificial offering?

Chuck Swindoll

"As each one has received a special gift, employ it in serving one another as good stewards of the manifold grace of God." (1 Peter 4:10)

A Place Just for You

Of all the places in the world, where do you think growing closer to God is the easiest? The church seems like a logical answer. After all, you talk and learn about God at church, and you're with people who feel similarly about Him. But if you'd like to grow in your relationship with God at church, it's more up to you than it is the pastor, programs, or Bible studies. The best way to see God's hand in your life is to find the specific place He desires you to serve in the body of Christ.

Find Your Fit

Read the following statements. Which one sounds most like you?

❑ I am patient, not prone to jumping into new ventures, but am willing to respond to others' needs quickly.

❑ I have an unusually strong desire to study God's Word.

❑ When I do something, I like to see the tangible results of my efforts.

❑ I spend a great amount of time praying for other people.

❑ I would rather share the Gospel or give my testimony than do anything else.

❑ I develop several steps of actions to solve every problem.

❑ I am very protective of people under my care.

❑ I tend to be incredibly perceptive when discerning other people's motives and purposes.

❑ When there is no leadership in a group, I will assume it.

❑ I have a compelling desire to see others learn and grow.

43

❏ I have a clear understanding of the Gospel and can easily relate it to others.

❏ I am already helping people when others are still talking about what to do.

Make Ministry Your Own

Did you find yourself responding "That's me!" to a few of the above statements? You may already sense where God has gifted you. You may find that you have the gift commonly called "service gifts," which includes skills such as administration, faith, and helping. Perhaps you're most comfortable fit is found in "support gifts," such as teaching or evangelism.

Be open to discovering something new about yourself—you just may be surprised! If you think you're only the behind-the-scenes type, try teaching a children's Sunday school class—you may be the perfect one for that ministry. Just as it's easier to steer a moving car, it'll be easier for you to find your perfect fit if you first try out a variety of ministries.

Once you discover your areas of strength and giftedness, the adventure has only begun. Don't just store your newfound tool in the garage—get out and use it! Make it a lifetime goal to practice it, learn about it, and talk with others about how to apply it to its maximum potential. As you experience all that the Lord wants to do in you and through you, your joy and excitement will only increase. Your gratitude to God and confidence that He is using you for a purpose that perfectly matches your abilities and skills will draw you closer to Him.

So, go ahead! Step out in faith, expecting God to direct you to the place of ministry He has prepared especially for you. Remember, "The body is not one member, but many. . . . God has placed the members, each one of them, in the body, just as He desired" (1 Corinthians 12:14,18). Isn't it time you discovered where God desires to use you?

The Practice of Prayer

My Father,

We know that people are watching Your church. They are listening to our words and evaluating how we treat each other and how we treat them. Please help us represent You. Help the grace that resides within us extend outward, touching lives.

Begin this work of grace in my own heart. Specifically, begin this work with my own tongue. Truth alone can be a bit harsh and abrasive, and I am occasionally too sharp when I speak before thinking. Give me the grace needed to cushion my words so that the truth may be received without needless offense.

Help us to appreciate each other for the gifts we can uniquely contribute—the pieces of Your divine puzzle that no one else can supply.

Grow our church deep as we dive into worship and instruction. Make our impact broad as we reach out in fellowship and evangelism. Help us to share Your Light with a dark world. Begin today, Lord, with me. Amen.

Make It Practical

As a believer, God's Spirit has given you at least one specific way to serve the body of Christ—it's called *your spiritual gift*. They are listed in the following verses:

- Romans 12:6–8
- 1 Corinthians 12
- Ephesians 4:7–16
- 1 Peter 4:10–11

Every believer, regardless of his or her gift, has the privilege of serving the body of Christ with . . .

- A ready, easy smile that greets somebody new or unfamiliar
- A flexible attitude and a good sense of humor for those unplanned detours in life
- A supportive heart toward others that celebrates differences
- A godly perspective that sees the value of the moment in view of eternity
- A fervent desire to do all for the glory of God

Directed Bible Study

GROWING CLOSER TO GOD THROUGH MINISTRY

Knowing your place in the body of Christ begins with knowing how God has personally gifted you. Discover and apply your gifts, and you will enjoy a personal ministry beyond your dreams!

1. Have you ever crafted a purpose statement for your life? It might be just what you need to stay on track in this busy world—and it serves as a tangible reminder of what God has called you to do with your life. Give it a try, and keep it simple—you can always refine and update your statement as you grow in your relationship with God.

The following questions have been provided to guide your thoughts:

- What do I do well? What do I love to do? When do I feel most fulfilled?

- What do my experiences tell me about my skills, interests, and dreams?

- How can God use my unique abilities for His glory?

My purpose statement:

2. Read 1 Corinthians 10:31. What purpose has God given to all Christians, regardless
   of their gifts, interests, or background? How does that purpose translate itself into
   your local church? Your small group? Your relationships?

3. Surprisingly, your pastor often finds himself a neglected member of the body of Christ, usually because the members of the church believe his needs are fulfilled by the intimacy he shares with God. But no matter his level of understanding, God desires "that the members may have the same care for one another" (1 Corinthians 12:25), which means that your pastor needs the fellowship of the body of Christ just as much as you do! Consider ministering to him in one of the following ways:

- *Compliment a specific strength*

- *Speak highly of him to others*

- *Show loyalty*

- *Submit to his leadership*

- *Provide for his material needs*

Want to discover your spiritual gift? The only way to find it is to jump into ministry of all kinds. When does success come naturally? In what areas do people affirm you? Start there, and have fun discovering the ways God can best use you.

8

GROWING CLOSER TO GOD
through
BIBLE STUDY

*As you get to know the people of the Bible
and see how God worked in their lives,
your anticipation for the future will grow.
Beyond the tangled trials of yesterday and the
present mess that puzzles you, you will find
hope by claiming the truths of Scripture—
a hope that will give you strength for
tomorrow's challenges.*

If I could have one wish granted for all of God's people, it would be that we return to the Word of God. The Bible is the final resting place for our hopes, our sorrows, and our surprises. As God uses life to teach us about the meaning of His Word, He then uses His Word to teach us about the meaning of life. If it weren't for His Book, we wouldn't know that Jesus loves us. That is our most profound hope, and that is the truth.

Chuck Swindoll

"Be diligent to present yourself approved to God as a workman who does not need to be ashamed, accurately handling the word of truth." (2 Timothy 2:15)

Do-It-Yourself Bible Study

Great craftsmen have long promoted the benefits of a do-it-yourself project. You design it to your own taste. You do it in your own time, as resources allow, and as your expertise grows. With good instructions and a willingness to learn, you're on your way to crafting a personal masterpiece.

When you engage in a do-it-yourself Bible study, you study the Masterpiece of all time—at your own pace, as your time allows, and in a way that satisfies your personal needs. By far, the best benefit of studying the Bible on your own is growing closer to the Master Craftsman as you understand His unique design for your life.

We asked Chuck Swindoll, "How have you designed your personal Bible study?" Simply stated, he starts with three key words and questions:

• **Look** at what the text says (observation). Look at words, pull out the dictionary, and trace their meanings. Compare that word with a similar word found another place in Scripture.

• **Ask** yourself, "What does this mean?" (interpretation). Finding answers to your questions will sometimes require that you meditate on the passage as well as reference good study Bibles and books.

• **Live** it out (application). What does the passage mean for you personally? What attitude, perspective, or actions should you adopt?

"I carry a yellow tablet with me wherever I go," Chuck said. "At home, at the office—I've even carried one in the car. I am forever working through these steps as they relate to a Bible passage. I've used these questions for four decades when I'm digging into the Scriptures."

Follow this in-progress Bible study, and discover how Chuck's three steps apply to the passage below.

Psalm 18:1-3

For the choir director. A Psalm of David the servant of the Lord, who spoke to the Lord the words of this song in the day that the Lord delivered him from the hand of all his enemies and from the hand of Saul. And he said,

¹"I love You, O Lord, my strength."

²The Lord is my rock and my fortress and my deliverer,

My God, my rock, in whom I take refuge;

My shield and the horn of my salvation, my stronghold.

³I call upon the Lord, who is worthy to be praised,

And I am saved from my enemies.

Look

Read 1 Samuel 24 for background. This song is also repeated in
 2 Samuel 22.

Who is the author?

Take note: This is a victory song!

How do the repeated metaphors found in this psalm describe God?

Take note: The repeated words *my* and *I* make this a very personal
 psalm.

Verse 3: My action—God's response.

Who are David's enemies? Why are they after him?

Ask

What did this song mean to David?

Where and why else did David compose a song to God?

Why is this Psalm repeated in 2 Samuel 22?

What is the core message of this passage?

Live

What does this psalm mean to me?

What timeless principles can be applied to my life?

Are cautions given? Words of encouragement?

What I've Learned

- I can be encouraged by God's protection of David.
- I can learn how to follow David's example of gratitude and worship.
- I can trust God's character as my rock, fortress, and shield, even when times are difficult.

Your Bible Study Toolbox

Discover insight into your questions and observations about a Bible passage with these tools:

- **A study Bible:** provides essential cross-references and context notes
- **Commentaries:** references that help explain books of the Bible
- **Concordance:** an alphabetical listing of all the Bible's words
- **Bible dictionary:** an alphabetical listing of key concepts, people, places, themes, and more
- **Bible atlas:** maps that give you an understanding of historical geography

The Practice of Prayer

Faithful God,

Your Word is such a source of comfort. In a calm, clear manner You have spoken so that Your words leave me encouraged. Thank You for replacing my fears with confidence, for removing my ignorance to make room for the reliable information I needed to know.

Thank You for composing Your Word so that I can understand it and for gracing it with variety and beauty and color. You've preserved it from error so that I can count on it. Please, Father, help me do that today.

In a new way today, teach me that there is no other foundation for life other than what You have laid in Your precious Word. How firm it is! Thank You, Father, for its consistent and constant direction that leads me to know Jesus Christ in a new and deeper way.

In a world where insecurity abounds, thank You for Your Word and for the confidence it gives concerning my secure foundation in Christ. Amen.

Make It Practical

As God's Word takes deeper root in your life, you can assume confidence in its authenticity for the following reasons:

- **Jesus did.** The Gospel of Matthew records that Christ taught and alluded to Scripture more than one hundred times.

- **The Resurrection.** The resurrection of Christ is the pivotal point of history, and the truth of Scripture is affirmed through it.

- **One common story.** Spanning forty generations and forty authors, the pages of Scripture unravel God's redemption of humanity.

- **Changed lives.** God's Word has influenced lives to bring growth to His church throughout history.

- **Integrity and accuracy.** God has protected Scripture so that nothing can or ever will disprove it.

- **It outlasts time.** God has promised that His Word will endure forever. (See Isaiah 40:8.)

Directed Bible Study

GROWING CLOSER TO GOD THROUGH BIBLE STUDY

The psalmist David loved God's Word more than his most valuable possession, calling it "more precious than gold" (Psalm 19:10 NIV). As you grow closer to God, the relevance of God's Word will grow in your life as well. The following exercises will help you gain more knowledge of and increase your love for God's Word.

1. The Psalms record a number of reflections upon the value of God's Word in our lives. In the left column below, list the characteristics of God's Word found in Psalm 19:7–11. In the right column, record the promise about Scripture that these verses allow you to claim.

Characteristic	Promise

2. Which characteristic found in the above left column most surprises you? How does it help you regard the Bible in a new way?

3. God's Word is referenced in each of the 176 verses of Psalm 119, using words such as *precepts*, *testimonies*, *commandments*, and *ordinances*. Read through this psalm slowly, paying special attention to the commitment the psalmist makes to obey and love God's Word. Note and perhaps memorize the verses that hold special meaning for you.

4. Are you keeping a steady diet with God's Word—savoring its truths, allowing time for it to digest in your soul, living out its application? Share with someone a significant verse or passage that has recently ministered to you. Be specific when communicating your appreciation for it.

In God's Word, you'll discover that the only way to grow in your relationship with God is through knowing His Son, the focal point of all Scripture.

9

GROWING CLOSER TO GOD
through
TRANSITIONS

Consider the roads your life has traveled.
No doubt you're facing circumstances today
that you hadn't expected to face five years ago,
five months ago, or even five days ago.
But remember, as life changes and you
experience various transitions, God is with you
and is working out His perfect plan in your life.

GROWING CLOSER TO GOD THROUGH TRANSITION:

A grasp of God's sovereignty
came to my rescue during
the hardest transitions of my life.
I've learned that in good times and
bad, His grace covers every
situation. God, and God alone,
is in full control.

Chuck Swindoll

"Nevertheless I am continually with You; You have taken hold of my right hand. With Your counsel You will guide me, And afterward receive me to glory."
(Psalm 73:23–24)

Detours and Other Adventures: Life on the Road

You know how it goes. You're cruising along in life, and suddenly the road takes a sharp turn. Perhaps the road signs warned you. Perhaps it comes by surprise. In either case, life will never be the same.

As you continue to focus on growing closer to God, glean wisdom from the testimonies below. They've been shared by friends of Insight for Living whose travels down life's winding roads have drawn them closer to God. Whether or not you've encountered these same detours, it is our hope that you will be encouraged by their words to strengthen your trust in God when you face a bend in the road.

Parents in Transition: Discovering Unconditional Love

"When we brought Jacob home from the hospital, we felt nothing but the excitement every first-time parent feels," share Marshall and Lauren Johnson. "But after six months, we noticed that Jacob wasn't progressing normally."

"We thought something was wrong," says Lauren, "but the doctors had no answers. For a year, we prayed and questioned doctors, friends, and God.

"We pleaded for answers. 'Why, God?' we asked. 'Why Jacob? Why us?' The transition from 'normal' parenting moved from disbelief to anger to bargaining, and finally to acceptance as our worst fears were confirmed: Jacob's life on earth would be brief due to a rare genetic disorder that inhibits normal development.

"To the doctors' amazement, God allowed us to care for Jacob another four years. They were the most significant four years of our lives."

"I grew to know what unconditional love is," Marshall says, "and how to depend on God's

59

strength when my physical, mental, and emotional strength is gone."

"Jacob taught us how to love," Lauren adds quietly. "When you loved him, you saw what God sees in us. We're His children. It was right to pour ourselves into loving Jacob."

"We realized early on that we could go two ways," says Marshall. "We could bury our heads in the sand and close ourselves off in our grief, or we could step out and help others. We found other families—many were Christians—who had children that were similarly affected. When we got together, our common bond was in Christ, not in the fact that our children were sick.

"We learned most of all that we are not in control. God has a plan even when things look like a mistake. Sometimes you just have to seek that plan out."

"When life seemed dark and gray, I repeated Isaiah 55:8–9," Lauren reflects. "God tells us, 'This plan of mine is not what you would work out, neither are my thoughts the same as yours! For just as the heavens are higher than the earth, so are my ways higher than yours, and my thoughts than yours' (LB).

"We found comfort and hope in trusting in God's ways."

Note: In February 2000, God brought a beautiful adopted daughter named Heather into Marshall and Lauren's hearts and home.

Motherhood in Transition: New Hope for the Empty Nest

"Motherhood is the one job that, if you do it well, you'll be out of a job," Linda Howington says with a smile. "So when my son and daughter both left for college, my nest was empty, and I felt unemployed. I loved being a hands-on mom. Their transition to college meant that I transitioned to being just a checkpoint in their lives.

"I dreaded having to let them go, so I had to learn to commit them to the Lord. I've learned never to get out of bed without praying for them. My prayer journal is my best tool—it's very comforting. I write a line for each one of us, then close it up and give them totally to the Lord. It's the only thing I can do for them, now that they're grown up.

"I had friends at church who were in my same boat, so we formed a Moping Moms Club. We get together every Saturday morning from 9:00 A.M. to 11:00 A.M., sometimes to walk or get coffee, or to teach each other something new. At first, our time was spent comforting each other. Now, we're excited about what we're doing with our new freedom.

"We also keep each other accountable. Instead of losses, we focus on joys. Sure, we let each other go through little periods of wallowing now and then, but at a certain point, we have to say, 'Okay, it's time to move on. What have you learned through this situation?' It would be hard to change the focus like this on your own. It helps to have a trusted friend who can jump-start your attitude.

"The biggest surprise in this transition has been the change in my relationship with the Lord and with my husband. Bob and I had stayed in our church because our kids had a great support group; once they left, we picked a church where we could grow. We're thrilled to be learning and even teaching and ministering to others. Growing closer to God together is the greatest thing that has ever happened to our marriage."

Faith in Transition: Healing from Loss

"I fundamentally believe that nothing happens in my life that He doesn't allow," Jeri Roesch says confidently. "I've been a Christian for thirty years, yet these last five years have marked the most challenging season in my life.

"One loss has followed another. I lost a home to a flood, my mom to cancer, my dad joined her in heaven two years later, a serious romantic relationship ended, and now a wonderful job is ending. On the horizontal plane, I realize that life happens. People get sick, homes get flooded, and change happens. But with a spiritual perspective, on the vertical plane, I know that He is aware of and has allowed these things to happen.

"One way that I've depended on God to heal my broken heart is to maintain my spiritual disciplines. Regardless of how I have felt at times, I've stayed involved at church, taken long prayer walks, and studied the Word. I've basically asked God to help me—I just 'show up' daily and give Him access to reach me, to speak to me, and to give me guidance.

"I've counted on the truths in Psalm 62:8: 'Trust in Him at all times, O people; Pour out your heart before Him.' He's invited me to be totally candid before Him, and I've found Him to be absolutely faithful with His presence.

"This doesn't mean that I have always seen clear, tangible 'solutions' in my life. When I was younger, the thing taken away would often be replaced by something else. But that's not been the case during this season. The only One who has stayed is the Lord. My options during this time of major life transition have been to trust Him and to discover what He will do, both in my earthly circumstances and (more importantly) in my relationship with Him.

"My deeper sense of His nearness brings peace, and I feel sincerely enthusiastic about life."

Health in Transition: Remembering God's Faithfulness

"When I think of the word *transition*, I think of my experience with breast cancer," reflects Charlotte Stiehl. "While I knew that life is precious, I came to fully acknowledge that reality once I realized my time on this earth was totally in the Lord's hands.

"This realization caused me to evaluate my priorities, especially in relationship to my family, friends, and work, and to look at how and where I was using my talents. Suddenly, I needed to use each day wisely.

"My body went through quite a transition—there are many scars, and a part of me is missing. While reconstruction is wonderful, it isn't the same. When I feel the weight of that loss, I go to God's Word and to prayer to remain focused on spiritual beauty and not physical beauty. Sometimes, in the middle of the night, I still wake up fearful that the cancer will return. It is then that I especially sense His nearness to me. All of these changes have opened up new ways of thinking that I'm still learning.

"Because of the cancer, my husband and I retired earlier than we planned. We also chose to relocate across the country.

"This journey has presented many challenges for both my husband and me, but we continually return to God's faithfulness. He said He will never leave us. So be assured. You and I are never, never, never alone."

Transformed from the Inside

As a child of God, your entire Christian experience is made up of one transition after another, even without dramatic changes in your life. There are at least three ways God draws you closer to Himself during transition—*from the inside.*

Romans 8:29 specifically says that God the Father is committed to the constant transformation of your character so that you become conformed to the image of His Son.

James 1:22 gives the exhortation to be more than a hearer of the Word, but a doer of it also. This is your part: the transition of your attitude and behavior.

And finally, 1 Peter 1 teaches that you are a pilgrim on this earth. You are literally a citizen of heaven, just passing through this life, waiting for your hope to be fulfilled in Christ Jesus. You're in a transition between heaven and earth.

The Practice of Prayer

My Father,

There is no more important moment of my day than right now, when I say in the depths of my heart, "I acknowledge You, Christ, as my Lord. I reaffirm my commitment to follow You through life's transitions. All that I have and hope to be is Yours."

Father, help me release to You the things I've held on to—in fact, clutched. Give me peace as I follow You in a new direction. Help me to be open and willing, free from resentment and bitterness. Stay near to me, encourage and comfort me, and please quiet my fears. Reassure me that with You, all is safe, no matter what lies ahead. I rest in You. Amen.

Make It Practical

Include the following ten essentials in your day-to-day life when facing times of transition.

- **Find a refuge in prayer.** Go boldly, go often—go just as you are. (Hebrews 4:16)

- **Ask God questions, and listen for His answers.** God promises to reveal Himself when we diligently seek Him. (Jeremiah 29:13)

- **Be sensitive to your personal needs.** Commit to healthy eating, sleeping, and exercising habits. (1 Corinthians 3:16–17)

- **Stay connected.** It's easy to isolate yourself. Instead, reach out to others. (1 Corinthians 12:26)

- **Keep laughing.** Look for the humor in everyday situations. (Proverbs 15:13)

- **Be wise.** Align your expectations with reality. (Proverbs 2:2–5)

- **Conserve your energy.** Listen for God's heartbeat in the midst of your circumstances, instead of resisting change. (Ecclesiastes 3)

- **Be grateful.** Give thanks to God for His many blessings each day. (Colossians 3:15)

- **Follow an example.** Seek out godly people who have gained wisdom from this same transition. (Proverbs 24:6)

- **Return to Scripture.** God's Word gives gentle reminders that you need not be afraid (Isaiah 43:1–3), that nothing will separate you from His love (Romans 8:38–39), and that He has prepared your path (Ephesians 2:10).

Directed Bible Study

GROWING CLOSER TO GOD THROUGH TRANSITIONS

During times of change, you are vulnerable to discouragement. Strengthen your heart by spending time in God's Word. When you meditate on His love for you, His provision becomes evident even in uncertain times.

1. Along the timeline of your life, what major events marked surprises or unexpected changes? When the unexpected happened to you, was God calling you to . . .

   • Release something or someone you loved, like Abraham? (Genesis 22)

   • Accept and endure mistreatment, like Joseph? (Genesis 37–49)

   • Wait patiently for something promised, like David? (Psalm 37)

   • Demonstrate some other act of faith?

During this trial, what did you learn about God? About yourself?

2. When you feel afraid to stop out in faith, it often helps to meditate on God's promises in Scripture. What biblical promise encourages you the most? Meditate on the following verses to strengthen your faith.

   • Psalm 23:4

   • Isaiah 41:10

   • Romans 8:31–39

• Hebrews 13:5–6

3. If you've been wrestling with God over the puzzling events in your life, remind yourself of His unchanging—and often mysterious—character. Read Job 11:7–9; Isaiah 55:8–9; and Romans 11:33–36. Write out your thoughts regarding those puzzling events, and release your anxiety to Him. When you do, you can claim Philippians 4:7.

Your place of safety during times of change will be in God's unchanging character. As James 1:17 promises, with God, "there is no variation or shifting shadow."

10

GROWING CLOSER TO GOD
through
PRAYER

Worship, surrender, petition, confession, and thanksgiving. Though your conversations with God may include much more, let Jesus' model of interaction with His Father form the framework of your prayers. Follow the Master Teacher as you grow closer to God through prayer.

The best kind of prayer is
done when no one is watching
or listening. It begins in the
closet, not at the church.
It bares its soul without
a hidden agenda. It genuinely
seeks to know what God desires.

Chuck Swindoll

*"In the morning I will order my prayer to
You and eagerly watch." (Psalm 5:2)*

If You Could Ask Jesus to Teach You One Thing . . .

As Christians, very few of us need to be persuaded of the importance of prayer. The real question is *how?* How should we pray? For what should we pray? How do we grow closer to God through prayer?

The Gospels capture a very endearing moment in Jesus' life that sheds light on this question. In Luke 11, Jesus was finishing a private conversation with His Father when "one of His disciples said to Him, 'Lord, teach us to pray'" (v. 1).

Now, these guys were not unschooled in religious rhetoric. No doubt they had been taught proper Jewish prayers since childhood. But Jesus prayed differently. As they overheard His prayers or prayed along with Him, their desire to pray more *like* Him increased. Ironically, they asked God Incarnate to tutor them in growing closer to God, His Father.

Let's sit at Jesus' feet with the disciples to learn a timeless lesson about how, and for what, we should pray. As recorded in Matthew 6, Jesus began His instruction in Heaven:

> ***Our Father who is in heaven,
> hallowed be Your name.***

Worship

Jesus modeled that our first appropriate thought in prayer should be to worship God for who He is— He is holy, and He is our Father. When we acknowledge God for who He is, our hearts melt in awe and adoration. Though in heaven, God desires to dwell with us here and now on earth. Though He alone is holy, His eagerness to connect with us is found in the gift of His Son. Heaven and earth join in this simple first statement.

Notes

69

Your kingdom come. Your will be done, on earth as it is in heaven.

Surrender

Jesus' instruction, as well as the example of His life, modeled surrender. The disciples heard Him pray these words not only on a Galilean hillside, but also in the garden outside Jerusalem as He prayed through the most painful night of His life. *Your will be done.* Jesus lived His entire life in surrender to His Father's will. He calls us to do the same.

Give us this day our daily bread. . . . And do not lead us into temptation, but deliver us from evil.

Petition

Just so that our prayers will be rooted in real living, Jesus reminded the disciples that we are dependent on God for everything—for today's food, for our next breath. He invites us to ask the Father for everything and anything according to His desire. In fact, even the word *prayer* means *to ask earnestly.* Jesus' example tells us to ask for God's protection against evil and for His provision of daily bread.

And forgive us our debts, as we also have forgiven our debtors.

Confession

Jesus lived with people long enough to get right to a root reason many prayers rise only ceiling-high: forgiveness. It's such an amazing gift from God and such a huge hurdle in our relationships with others! But Jesus addressed the issue head-on. In essence, He said that the effectiveness of your prayers depends upon your willingness to forgive someone else. (Anyone come to mind?)

For Yours is the kingdom and the power and the glory forever.
Amen.

Thanksgiving

When we acknowledge God to be the Author of all life, all blessing, all kingdoms, and all glory, Jesus said He is duly honored. Everything we have, we received from His hand. There is no better way to pray than to thank Him for all He is—the Focus of all eternity. Jesus directs our response toward pure thanksgiving.

The Practice of Prayer

Teach me, Father, what it means to know You and Your Son deeply and intimately. Remove whatever distraction keeps me from spending much of my time with You. Help me to make my conversations with You one of my greatest priorities.

Forgive me, Lord, when I've taken the complicated way through life instead of the plan You had already established for me. Give me eyes to see and a heart to understand Your will for me. Replace my doubts with a willingness to trust You, and help me be confident in Your faithfulness.

Father in heaven, I give You thanks for being so good. Thank You for allowing me to approach You boldly in prayer because of Jesus' sacrifice. May my prayers be like a sweet fragrance when they rise before Your throne. Thank you for Your love and for Your Son. Amen.

Make It Practical

What does the Lord's Prayer mean to you?

When you say:	It means:
Father	You have accepted His Son as your Savior.
Hallowed be Your name	You praise His character.
Your kingdom come	You commit to be a part of its development.
Your will be done	You surrender your agenda.
On earth as it is in heaven	You proclaim His salvation to the world.
Give us this day our daily bread	You accept all things from His hand.
Forgive us our trespasses	You resolve conflicts quickly.
Lead us not into temptation	You desire integrity in your own life.
Deliver us from evil	You put on the whole armor of God. (Ephesians 6:11)
Yours is the Kingdom	You submit to God's right over your life.
Yours is the power	You rely on God's strength.
Yours is the glory	You reflect praise to Him.
Forever	You look forward to an eternity in His presence.

Directed Bible Study

GROWING CLOSER TO GOD THROUGH PRAYER

Prayer is God's personal invitation to draw near to Him. In prayer, you can pour out your heart and listen to Him at the same time. In the following questions and exercises, focus on how you can better meet with Him in a fresh, personal way.

1. Take stock of your prayer life. What, if anything, needs to change? Spend a portion of your prayer time today with each of the following directives:

   • Express to God your love, worship, thanksgiving, and praise.

   • Ask God for help with your needs and others' needs.

   • Confess your sins.

   • Listen for His voice. What do you hear Him saying to you?

2. What frustrates you most about prayer? Right now, voice that frustration to God. He appreciates your honesty. Write out a prayer that expresses how you would like to see your prayer life grow. Pray it aloud or silently.

3. Try an experiment. Set aside 3–5 minutes for the next seven days to sit in a quiet place and focus your heart and mind on listening to God. If you become distracted by something you need to do, write it on a notepad and still your heart before God again. Attach your thoughts to one of the following lines of Scripture: "My peace I give you" (John 14:27); "Lo, I am with you always" (Matthew 28:20); "'God, be merciful to me'" (Luke 18:13); or a line from the Lord's Prayer (Matthew 6:9–13).

4. Read the following passages and record what you learn from the psalmists' attitudes and methods of approaching God:

  • Psalm 130:5–6

  • Psalm 62:1–2

  • Psalm 63:1–6

  • Psalm 19:14

As you pray, observe how God is working in the lives and circumstances around you. Do you see Him answering your requests? Making provision for you? Causing new growth? "See that the Lord is good" (Psalm 34:8).

GROWING CLOSER TO GOD
through
EVANGELISM

*The prospect of reaching every person in every
nation with the Gospel is overwhelming
sometimes. And you know what the Lord says
in response to those fears? "One person
at a time." Your faithfulness to sharing the
Good News with one person at a time will
pave the way for ministry that makes a
difference in eternity.*

When you've won a hearing, when you've arrested the attention of another because you're different than the masses, remember that the word is Jesus. It's not about church or baptism, or even about dropping an addiction. People are saved by the Good News of Jesus Christ alone. And when they've decided they want to follow Jesus, move forward. Take action and tell them how to receive God's gift of salvation.

Chuck Swindoll

> *"Always be prepared to give an answer to everyone who asks you to give the reason for the hope that you have." (1 Peter 3:15b NIV)*

Your Turn: How to Share the Best Thing That's Ever Happened to You

God has provided an open door. A conversation with a friend, an acquaintance, or a family member turns to spiritual questions, and suddenly you find yourself with an opportunity to explain what having a relationship with God really means.

What should you do now?

If you've ever been in this situation, you may have:

a. Eagerly explained the Gospel using the Romans Road or the Four Spiritual Laws.

b. Offered a watered-down, cliché-filled explanation of the Gospel so as not to offend their beliefs.

c. Told them that you'd ask your pastor to call them at his earliest convenience.

d. Run.

No matter where your comfort level rests in terms of personal evangelism, the reality is that God has opened this door of opportunity, and He desires to use you to change someone's life. Incredible thought, isn't it?

How can you do that? Formulas, techniques, and strategies aside, perhaps the most valuable way for you to share the best thing that's ever happened to you is to tell your own story. Share candidly and personally with your friend or family member how your life has changed since you gave your life to Christ.

Tell Your Personal Story

A testimony is simply a firsthand account. When you tell someone your testimony, you open your life to them in a non-threatening way—you explain who Jesus Christ is and the personal difference He has made in your life. When you give evidence as to how the power of God has transformed your life, you illustrate one instance of the miracle of salvation. Even if your testimony isn't filled with fireworks and tragedy, it's a miracle.

People are looking for evidence that God exists and that He is personally involved in individual lives. Your story proves that God wants to know you . . . and them. More than a formula or technique, evangelism is a way of living—of being available to God in the opportunities He gives us.

Preparing Your Story

When the time comes to share your personal testimony with a friend, you can be certain that the Holy Spirit will be working in your mind and heart, giving you discernment in what to say. However, long before that conversation begins, you need to organize your thoughts. Just as a lawyer would not walk into a courtroom unprepared, you shouldn't approach your testimony on "a wing and a prayer." Plan your story with these three points in mind:

1. **Remember your purpose.** You want to let others know what Christ has done in *your* life. Edit out personal details that nudge your audience in ways you think they need to change or that offer pat answers to life's critical questions. Focus on how God changed you and what He's done.

2. **Build common bridges.** Explain your story so that the person can identify with your past and present experiences. Give examples of how God has fulfilled His promise that, "If anyone is in Christ, he is a new creation; the old has gone, the new has come!" (2 Corinthians 5:17 NIV) Admit openly that God is still working in your life, still changing your life for good.

3. **Keep it simple.** You might tell your story by sharing about three life moments—before Christ, the birth of Christ in your life, and after Christ. The last thing you'd want to do is make a simple message unclear or difficult—a person's attention span usually lasts about three minutes. So, keep it short and focused.

Lessons from Your Story

Even if an opportunity to share your testimony doesn't present itself soon, the practice of reflecting on how God has been at work in your life will yield wonderful benefits. It's easy to forget how faithful God has been, isn't it? Too often we forget that God's story is continuing to unfold in our lives. When you remember His goodness in directing your life's path, you'll be moved toward a lifestyle of gratitude, worship, greater intimacy with God, and greater trust in God. People are bound to notice how different you are, and they'll be drawn to ask you, "What's your secret?"

The Practice of Prayer

My Father,

For just one moment, let me imagine what it would be like to live this entire day knowing nothing of peace with You, having nothing but fear and superstition wrapping its clammy arms around me, not knowing my destination if I were to take my last breath. Help me to remember what it was like before I knew You and to keep that desperation in mind when I'm presented with an opportunity to share the hope of the Gospel.

I commit myself anew as Your ambassador. This year, Lord, use me to reach one person with Your saving grace. May my relationship with them grow to such a point that You allow me to be part of their amazing process of salvation.

Thank You, Father, for continuing to convict me of sin and for drawing me to Yourself. Open my lips to speak openly and freely and joyfully and authentically of the Christ who has come into my life. For this I give You thanks. Amen.

Make It Practical

When Jesus shared the Good News, He met people on their turf—tax collectors, adulterers, well-educated leaders, little children, physically impaired men and women, and common laborers. He often began His conversations by asking questions—and then He listened carefully to their answers. (See John 4.)

Philip used the same model in Acts 8 when he chanced upon the Ethiopian official reading from the Old Testament. He asked, "Do you understand what you are reading?"

You can follow their model today by learning to ask the right questions, listen to their answers, and respond to the needs before you. When you find yourself with an open door of opportunity, use one of these questions to get the conversation started:

• What is it that you think the world needs more than anything else?

• Do you ever wish you could make a fresh start in life?

• What do you think will make people successful in the 21st century?

• What do you think people mean when they say they know God?

Directed Bible Study

GROWING CLOSER TO GOD THROUGH EVANGELISM

The question "When's the last time you shared your faith?" can strike a chord of guilt in the most devout Christian. Most of us would love to tell more people about Jesus Christ, but some of us lack confidence, while others fear rejection. Some don't feel they're living a lifestyle worthy of sharing, while others simply don't know how. No matter the reason, you can begin sharing your faith with the help of the exercises below.

1. Have you ever written out your personal testimony? Give it a try! Tell it simply, without using a lot of Christian vocabulary, so that people can easily understand what has made a difference in your life. You may want to practice delivering it, along with the Gospel message, to an honest but sensitive friend.

2. Read the following verses, and make a list of the key elements to include in a Gospel presentation.

    Acts 26:16–18

    1 Corinthians 15:1–11

    Ephesians 2:1–10

3. Why do you think most people who hear the Gospel resist embracing it? Make a list of five reasons you've heard or experienced, and then think through a sensitive, reasonable response to each objection. Review 1 Peter 3:15 for encouragement.

4. Think of someone that you know who needs to hear about Christ. What obstacles make it difficult for you to talk to that person about God's truth? List two or three ways you can build a bridge of understanding with that person.

When you share the message of salvation, remember that people have two kinds of needs—what they know they need (such as emotional relief and the solutions to life's problems) and what they actually need (such as forgiveness of sins, access to God, and eternal salvation). Ask God for wisdom to respond to the emotional and spiritual needs of those around you.

GROWING CLOSER TO GOD
through
TRADITIONS

*Traditions make celebrations more meaningful
and personal; they allow us to celebrate in
ways that are uniquely ours. However, when
we rejoice without the Savior, we detract from
the true cause for celebration—the new life
we have in Christ. As you place Him at the
center of each holiday and tradition,
you will radiate a joy that is tangible,
meaningful, and contagious.*

GROWING CLOSER TO GOD THROUGH TRADITIONS

One of this world system's most effective maneuvers creates a false sense of excitement in the anticipation of the holiday seasons. The afterglow of each celebration can be a dangerous, depressing experience. Guard yourself. Enjoy the time of merriment . . . but not at the expense of what's to come. Make Hebrews 12:3 your aim—consider Him.

Chuck Swindoll

"A festival or a new moon or a Sabbath day . . . are a mere shadow of what is to come; but the substance belongs to Christ." (Colossians 2:16–17)

Celebrating Jesus

During the Christmas season, we celebrate Jesus and the access to God we have through Him. Eugene Peterson's *The Message* describes Jesus' incarnation in this refreshing way:

> The Word became flesh and blood, and moved into the neighborhood. We saw the glory with our own eyes, the one-of-a-kind glory, like Father, like Son, generous inside and out, true from start to finish.

Want to make each Christmas season one to remember? Consider how to move into the neighborhood with your celebration. Help people know God's love during that season by being generous inside and out, true from start to finish. Jesus' names, so familiar to the Christmas season, give us insight into how to model His character to our world.

Isaiah predicted Jesus' birth in Bethlehem, referring to Him as . . .

The Prince of Peace (Isaiah 9:6)

You hear a lot about peace on earth at Christmastime. But no matter the truce talks on the battlefields or in your home, you can't impose peace. Peace radiates from the inside out—it follows when the heart is at rest with God. Consider the things that churn in your heart this season. Questions or decisions may weigh heavily on your mind. Relationships may be out of sync. With faith, surrender these needs to Your Father. He promises that He will keep "in perfect peace [literally, *shalom*] him whose mind is steadfast, because he trusts in [Him]" (Isaiah 26:3 NIV).

Bethlehem's angel announced that Jesus was . . .

The Savior, Who Is Christ the Lord (Luke 2:11)

As our Savior, Jesus came "to seek and to save that which was lost" (Luke 19:10). You can model this initiative during the Christmas season by seek-

85

ing out people who, because of a conflict or a lack of time, have become distant. If forgiveness is needed, then offer it or receive it with grace. Certainly the cost or effort may be high, but you will thrill at how God redeems, or buys back, that valuable relationship for you. Model Christ this season by redeeming relationships with people who are important to you and to God.

Jesus Himself said He was . . .

The Light of the World (John 9:5)

Don't you love to look at Christmas lights around your community? Ever notice that it's in darkness that their beauty shines best? The same is true for you. You best reflect Jesus, the Light of the World, when you shine for Him *in the world*. Perhaps Christmas is the perfect time for you to share with your neighbor the hope you have in Christ. Or consider volunteering at your local women's shelter or looking into any number of opportunities available through your church or in your community. Grasp every occasion the season offers to share the light of Christ with someone walking in darkness.

The angel told Joseph that Mary's child would be called . . .

Immanuel: God with Us (Matthew 1:23)

After the holidays pass, Jesus' name, *Immanuel,* reminds you that you're not alone. Jesus remains "God with you." You can model this reality as you deal with life's most difficult moments. Who in your life needs to hear that God has not left him or her alone to face life's challenges? A lonely parent? A struggling teenager? Consider the most effective way to communicate that encouragement to them. This reminder of God's presence could be the most important present you give.

When December's highs and lows settle into January's predictable pace, gifts and gatherings will dim from memory. But what you will remember is how God's gifts became more personal and practical. You'll remember how you modeled Jesus, who moved into the neighborhood so people could see His grace and glory with their own eyes.

The Practice of Prayer

Lord,

Thank you for today—for its uniqueness! It has never occurred before, and it will never be repeated. At midnight it will end . . . quietly, suddenly, totally. Forever. But the hours between now and then are opportunities with eternal possibilities.

Thank You for the remembrance that special days bring. Thank You for the day we remember Your Son's incarnation. Thank You for those solemn and celebratory days we remember Your Son's sacrificial gift on Calvary.

And thank You for making each day a gift from You—another opportunity to live for You and to remember and celebrate all that You have done for us. Please remind me to look for Your grace in each day and to number each one as I apply my heart to gaining wisdom. Lord of my days, I commit to follow You today and for the rest of my life. Amen.

A Closing Thought

Christmas offers a wonderful message: *Immanuel*, "God with us." He who resided in Heaven, coequal and coeternal with the Father and the Spirit, willingly descended into our world. He breathed our air, felt our pain, knew our sorrows, and died for our sins. He didn't come to frighten us, but to show us the way to know His Father. May the warmth of the Savior's love spread itself over you as never before, and may you, whenever possible, share in word and action the Good News of Christ with everyone you meet.

Directed Bible Study

GROWING CLOSER TO GOD THROUGH TRADITIONS

What is a holiday except a specific time set aside to remember and celebrate? Of course, the two most significant holidays for Christians are Christmas, when we celebrate our Lord's arrival, and Easter, when we remember and celebrate His sacrificial gift of salvation. But there are also hundreds of days in between to celebrate His other gifts. Read on to discover how to grow closer to God through times of remembrance.

Easter

- The central message of the Bible is encapsulated in the Cross. As you read the following passages that describe the significance of Christ's death on the cross, ask yourself these questions: What does this verse teach about Christ's sacrifice? What does that personally mean to me?

  Matthew 26:28

  Romans 5:9

  Galatians 3:13

  Ephesians 2:14–16

Colossians 1:19–20

Colossians 2:13–15

Hebrews 9:14

1 Peter 1:18–19

1 John 1:7

Revelation 5:9

- Write a letter to a friend—real or imaginary—who has recently come to the saving knowledge of Jesus Christ, and describe all that the Cross has accomplished for them.

Christmas

- Christ's incarnation had been expected hundreds of years before the angel announced His arrival in Bethlehem. In order to fully appreciate the names that have been ascribed to Him, such as Messiah and Christ, trace the original prophecies to their fulfillment in Jesus. Read the verses in each section and then draw a line from the prophecy to the passage that fulfills it.

Birth

Prophecy	Fulfillment
Isaiah 7:14	Luke 1:32–33
Jeremiah 23:5	Matthew 2:1, 11
Psalm 72:10	Matthew 1:18, 24–25

Life

Prophecy	Fulfillment
Isaiah 11:2	Luke 19:35–37a
Isaiah 35:5–6	Matthew 11:4–5
Zechariah 9:9	Matthew 3:16

Give Thanks

- Consider the spiritual significance of each holiday you celebrate, and praise God for His gift to you on that day. Make a list below of those days and for what you can specifically thank Him. For example, on Valentine's Day, you can thank God for His love for you; on Memorial Day, you can remember those who have died for their faith.

Growing closer to God requires a lifetime journey toward His throne. Dedicate the rest of the years God gives you to knowing and loving Him more intimately. May your heart's song continually resound with this chorus: "Oh, the depth of the riches both of the wisdom and knowledge of God!" (Romans 11:33).

Ordering Information

If you would like to order additional resources from Insight for Living, please contact the office that serves you.

United States and International locations:
Insight for Living
Post Office Box 69000
Anaheim, CA 92817-0900
1-800-772-8888, 24 hours a day, seven days a week
(714) 575-5000, 8:00 A.M. to 4:30 P.M., Pacific time, Monday to Friday

Canada:
Insight for Living Ministries
Post Office Box 2510
Vancouver, BC, Canada V6B 3W7
1-800-663-7639, 24 hours a day, seven days a week
infocanada@insight.org

Australia:
Insight for Living, Inc.
20 Albert Street
Blackburn, VIC 3130, Australia
Toll-free 1800 772 888 or (03) 9877-4277, 8:30 A.M. to 5:00 P.M.,
    Monday to Friday
iflaus@insight.org

World Wide Web:
www.insight.org